The Other Place

The Other Place

poems

Brendan Cleary

Pighog Press | *Chester, U.K.*

Book layout by Daniela Connor

Library of Congress Cataloging-in-Publication Data

Names: Cleary, Brendan, author.
Title: The other place : poems / Brendan Cleary.
Description: First edition. | Pasadena, CA : Pighog Press, [2021]
Identifiers: LCCN 2021000995 (print) | LCCN 2021000996 (ebook) | ISBN
  9781906309534 (trade paperback) | ISBN 9781906309565 (epub)
Subjects: LCGFT: Poetry.
Classification: LCC PR6053.L388 O84 2021 (print) | LCC PR6053.L388
  (ebook) | DDC 821/.914—dc23
LC record available at https://lccn.loc.gov/2021000995
LC ebook record available at https://lccn.loc.gov/2021000996

The National Endowment for the Arts, the Los Angeles County Arts Commission, the
Ahmanson Foundation, the Dwight Stuart Youth Fund, the Max Factor Family Foundation,
the Pasadena Tournament of Roses Foundation, the Pasadena Arts & Culture Commission
and the City of Pasadena Cultural Affairs Division, the City of Los Angeles Department of
Cultural Affairs, the Audrey & Sydney Irmas Charitable Foundation, the Meta & George
Rosenberg Foundation, the Albert and Elaine Borchard Foundation, the Adams Family
Foundation, Amazon Literary Partnership, the Sam Francis Foundation, and the Mara W.
Breech Foundation partially support Red Hen Press.

First Edition
Published by Pighog Press
an imprint of Red Hen Press
www.redhen.org/pighog

ACKNOWLEDGEMENTS

The author would like to thank the editors of the following publications in which some of these poems first appeared:

Echo Room Press: "Esme Letters," "Ghost Tapes," "Love Hotel Poems"; *Poetry N. Ireland*: "4x4"; and *Wivenbooks*: "Days Begin."

"Clean" was recorded with music from the sadly departed saxophonist Norbert Vollath at the Tyrone Guthrie Centre, Annagmakerigg, Ireland, in 2014.

"The Other Place" was performed with music from saxophonist Ken Marshall in Cork, Ireland, in 2018.

The author wishes to thank the following:

The Tyrone Guthrie Centre, Annaghmakerrig, Ireland; the Royal Literary Fund; the Society of Authors; The Great Eastern Public House, Brighton.

Peter Berman, Alex Brockhurst, Chris Butler, John Davies, Tom Holmes, Freya Hutchison, Majella Keller, Anthony MacKee, Les Robinson, Casper Slater, Jackie Wills, and Gary Zhexi Zhang.

i.m.

my family

Peggy Cleary

Martin Cleary Snr

Martin Cleary Jnr

CONTENTS

i

Ghost Tapes

ii

Esme Letters

iii

The Other Place

The Other Place

i

Ghost Tapes

Pucks Lane

past Haverons butchers
at the turn into something

past the Marine Bar
James & Molly at the fire

past the Rangers Club
where Paschal sometimes drank

past the Top Path
past the White Harbour

past Sunshine House
where Spike Milligan hung out

past the promenade spray
where Sting jammed with Niel

past the lighthouse cliffs
where Stephen fell

past the Garden Village
past the Wrens Eggs

past Pucks Lane
always at the edge of something

Last Christmas

aye it was about two years ago
about this time in the sun

you in the kitchen chair
as I worked at the cooker

chopping parsnips & spuds
turning the turkey over

following your instructions
'you cooked this not me'

I mentioned at the fire
but you hardly ate anything

& later dozed off
halfway through Emmerdale

Some Days

days without your cupboards
days without your spoons
without your brogue

or the slit in the blinds
as I glimpsed the rain
hard on Windsor Avenue

days without your soup
& some days holes so deep
I fall into them & swim

conjuring your face
or trying to hear the clock
chiming over your fireplace

Miss Brannagh

every night about nine
you went next door
to check her place
see if there were ghosts
or any intruders
under her curtains & beds
or behind her cupboards
& I remember going with you
in late summer twilight
smelling her old corners
watching new dust gather

Vertigo

after Bargain Hunt
I'll head to the bakery
for soup & baps

I'll stand by the sink
near the microwave
& you'll be in your chair

holding out your carton
to show me all the barley
you do this everytime

as trees out the window
at the edge of Brooklands
fall into our afternoon

Number 55

please don't think me strange
I used to live here
& would like to wander about
in the upstairs rooms

in my dreams I've counted
every step fom Mama's bedroom
up to mine & then Martin's
in the attic with the wardrobe outside

& you'll have changed the place
yet I won't mind
so long as you let me
breathe in my past again

Ghost Attic

strange to live in Ghost Attic
it's nothing like the attic
in the old house on Cable Road

Martin's room with the Subbuteo
& him playing Humble Pie albums
waiting for Pauline to call

or next door my old room
where Pat Haveron made shelves
for my stereo & books

& I'd always see you down in the yard
with the coal shovel
& a fag in your mouth

My Dada

that goal I scored
for the Black & Ambers
with Roger Coppock in nets
at Islandmagee's ground
has been spinning in my head
& it still does Dada

I still carry your thoughts
on the edge of you being there
& I want to walk down with you
to the old library in the dark
on Tuesday winter evenings
when I still felt safe

Ghost Tapes

ghost voices
in the wind
on Blackhead steps

ghost tales
at the back tables
of the Marine Bar

Wesley & Charlie
Shu Dick & old Sandy
all the lost ghosts

crying out again
as I walk in tears
over the station bridge

Ghost Pool

on the promenade
seaweed scattered

far from the railings
all over the place

near the Rangers Club
which was Ma Hambo's cafe

where I played pinball
& Christine took acid

& look! the dead pool
where Tim was lifeguard

& couldn't even swim
& Pip used to climb

up to the top board
& dive into the sea

Ghost Sun

"Pass the Dutchie"
on the transistor

& sunshine forever
on Cable Road

the tennis courts
the old Whitehead pitch

the reservoir at dawn
where the pills were hidden

the Raw Brae
the putting green

& Olive & Tracey Jones
still very beautiful

Ghost Dream

I'm on the Larne train
passing Cloghan Point

with the long pier
in the winter sun

& you've asked me
to pick up milk

on my way at Dickie's
before we hug on the porch

I put my bag away
in the back hall

you ask about the plane
'was it full?'

& take out my chop
kept warm in the oven

Your Vase

I really did think
keeping that vase
from your sideboard
on my window sill
on top of the Blues CDs
would help you stay
so now I want your saucepans
& the cat ornaments
I gave to Annette
& old scraps of paper
with your writing on as well

In Larne

maybe you'll find
a handbag you like
in the Cancer shop

we could get a fry
before Iceland
for your mints

& you'll have your stick
but I'll help you
let you take my arm

after your rest on the bench
in the shopping arcade
heading to the car park

In the Sky

give me the heat of a city
all my silent losses

give me rain under lights
at the greyhound track

give me the shipping forecast
all your burnt love letters

give me my Mama back
give me frost on hedges

give me a little more
in some January sky

ii

Esme Letters

1.

I knew there was one thing
I needed to do today
buy bog roll & I pulled it off

Esme do you ever get those days
when you feel like you're drowning
water everywhere & no more bread

pints in the afternoon
have become natural to me
it's become my job

2.

Esme I'm reliably informed
I'm not 'relationship material'

I think it's got something
to do with the drink & drugs
the constant gambling

& I've no reason to doubt
the folk who tell me this
but where does that leave us?

I can walk with you
down the avenue of trees
or I could whirl your soul
around a field like a frisbee

the frisbee of love Esme
the stars cry for your bones
I could eat your hair

but the council tax bill
the bungalow & the sofa bed
I'm uncertain about all of these things

3.

it was a stupid bet Esme
Doncaster to draw
& they're beaten 6-nil

'hell is other people'
said Sartre I believe
& the ten men of Oldham Athletic
fit into this theory

but there's a horse running tomorrow
that's in Tom's notebook
& this usually means
something good might happen

4.

a strange beam of light
cuts through the dark
this night as I dream

I know it's you Esme
so imagine you naked
or semi-naked at least

I know you're watching
& in the morning cafe
we'll kiss below the fire escapes

5.

Gordon jumped off a bridge
into the river at Durham

& Mama & Dada vanished
Big Facey died in his yard

Esme I hope it's OK
to tell you stuff like this

6.

I don't believe in fate
only heartache & hotels
where we'll end up Esme

Switzerland & Oslo Norway
the Railway Hotel in Newcastle
as the pale light collapses

& we wander to Chinatown
for Crispy Aromatic Duck
so please don't say you don't want this

7.

Esme I'm sliding down
en route with the Sauce Doctor

a long journey over trees
the light so extraordinary

but this wine has got a grip
so I'll get back to you tomorrow

Cafe Paris

you ask me to explain
the Deep Existential Void
in Cafe Sartre over espresso

but I flounder about
the clouds descending
offering no conclusion

& the side of your breast
enters my view at random
ordering another croissant

Our Rooms

just my own room now
& not yours nor the dawn
with the half-packet
of Rich Tea at your bedside

no only my room now
the Jimmie Rodgers CD
the ashtray of hash
& in the sketchbook your only photo

My Addictions

you know all about
my addictions
the dark arts
the black places
so there's no sense
in mentioning
the tea garden
that shed in the sun
& our eyes
alive with each other

Bird

in the kitchen I asked his advice
& he asked me in return
did I have 'a bird on the go?'

& it so happens I didn't
& may never again
have 'a bird on the go'

so I lied again
& told him about you
as if you were my girlfriend

Esme Remembered

yes I'll buy you
an eighteen-inch pizza
from Papa John's
any toppings you like!

OK you can have the last
of these pickled gherkins
& my old C90 compilations
if you give them back one day

& look! my life-size photo
of Anna Kournikova
is fading in this sun
your phone on silent again

Mike's Garden

near the rust
of the climbing frame
dilapidated
smoking the first
after last night

& I want to kiss
your sorry eyelids
wondering again
who you were
before you changed
your name

Mayday

just beside our table
in the Pavilion gardens
they dance about with beards

adjacent to our table
in the Pavilion gardens
their flesh full of spring

their bells all a-chiming
so it's just you & me now
waiting for Morris Men forever

Zurich

it occurs to me you lied
when you came back
from Zurich

& told me nothing happened
so please tell me who it was
for the record

because you definitely did it
I know that now
in the soles of my shoes

The Leaves

I knew in October
you'd go

but I didn't say
because of the leaves

& their messages
& the silver birch tree

Esme the Musical

our secret invisible orchestra
strikes up
Gershwin strings

& Jack & Jack & Janey
behind the bar
waltz & sing harmonies

it won't be long Esme
I can read it on your red lips
as the single trumpet mourns

aye it won't be long Esme
the horns & drums crescendo
& you head off to the carpark

iii

The Other Place

Clean

suddenly the prospect of bad blood
so the trees on the rise are friends
& I'd grow backwards if I only could
in case everything there is just ends

& it's not just the trees but the wind
I want it to blow through me & heal
all the hurt & bring back all my kin
from their dirty graves & guess I feel

the time has come to get myself clean
& walk in the garden with a pure heart
not the let the sorrows get in between
my daydreams of a fresh new start

& I'd grow backwards if I only could
through years & years of bad blood

1968

riding in the old Ford Anglia to Dundalk
all of us eating chips in the Roma Cafe
& my family who vanished well they walk
into the clouds away from me in a melee

of nothingness & vacuum & I want them to gather
go again on the old trips through loose chippings
the boys in the back seat smelling hot leather
but all I can see are the cold ripplings

of the backs of their capes disappearing
climbing some invisible ladder to heaven
Dada in the front seat doing the steering
& Mama beside him so now I can begin

I'll take my searchlight into that melee
all of us eating chips in the Roma Cafe

In Our Eyes

look at the young lovers hand in hand
their eyes half-full of eagerness
I'll follow them into some distant land
of lost hearts & if I could just caress

the sweet hairs of yesterday & the eyes
of girls on the bandstand & their smiles
when I was behaving & then the lies
I could see for miles & miles

I'll row with young lovers on the lake
instead of smoking in the bitter air
I'll show them delights & I'll make
their eyes glow with love & care

look at the young lovers hand in hand
I'll follow them to some distant land

Ghost Estate

you called me here
to the ghost estate

& in the gravel I walk
over the half-laid path

stand by the sink
without any taps

open the wardrobe
with only one door

& there are no radiators
just cement everywhere

as I stare out the only window
at the swaying trees

to where a roof should be
& hear you speak my name

Ghost Train

standing on the pier
with our ice cream

halfway between the Dolphin Derby
& the arcade with robots

one-armed bandits
& the horseracing machine

always your favourite
then our laughs on the Ghost Train

full of shrieks & moving screams
bats descending as we hurtle

& the witch with the crooked eyes
& the skeleton that drops

as if from hell or the sky
& brushes across your face

Conductor

if I end up
as a Conductor
I'd like to be
the Conductor
on the Darlington/
Saltburn line
in the late seventies

the happiest person
I've ever come across
& if he's still alive
he'll still be cheery
in the nursing home
still a martyr
for the entire world

everybody smiles with him
in the late seventies
on the Saltburn train
so if I do end up
as a Conductor
I have vast amounts
to live up to & learn

This Morning

could be worse this morning
sun near my heart again
on my way to the Clocktower

could be a lot grimmer
still here it seems
haven't been diagnosed

haven't been impaled on a spike
still kicking this morning
my heart not hurting yet

The High Stool

this is where
I feel the best
most of the time

no white powder
sad movies
tame excuses

it's my kingdom
this afternoon unreeling
from my deranged throne

Autumn Morning

it's 2022 a bright Autumn morning
& I'm gathering leaves hungover

leaves & sticks & branches
& I'm old working for Jon

cos he wouldn't see me skint
but I only do the picking up

& the sweeping nothing else
& it's kind of Jon the gardener

to give me work after I've spunked
all of my money on horses & drink

Burger Tuesday

bizarre coincidence
our very first nearly date
& this is Burger Tuesday

don't talk to me about relish
or offers on the blackboards
or the juice on my youth

Burger Tuesday fancy that!
& us here nearly kissing
like back in the old days

Dieppe

in another lifetime I told you
& low & behold you agreed

but have fled to Dieppe
carrying my I-Ching in your hold-all

in another ghost photograph
in another experimental video

in another Hollywood Blockbuster
sailing off to Dieppe

Deja Vu

she might be in Tangier
but more likely Gateshead

staggering under the weight
carting her children around

in Asda Lidl or Aldi
& every so often she remembers

with a mild electronic shock
from the toaster or microwave

the room decked out with incense
the pure sound of our jazz

The Guilt Ship

leaves from North Shields tomorrow
off it'll go over the waves to Norway

in the mist over Tynemouth castle
the guilt ship sailing out

miraculous colour in the skies
& the next dawn will cure us

it always does as we watch
the guilt ship sail away

Girl with Flier

thank you
I didn't expect this

in these wrinkles & sun
& my life has been varied

I've had loads of experienes
my lovemaking complimented

although there were also times
when I was far too drunk

August without Esme

sad for Sam Shepard
sad for Professor Fred Snow

sad for the dead leaves
sad for the troubling sea

sad for the November blues
sad for my door key

& no matter how much I pretend
I'm sad for lines around my eyes

the half-drunk pints
the ripped-up bookies slips

the sicknotes & Red Bulls
& all the many likes & dislikes

Things Esme didn't know

in the pub
near midnight
you didn't know
who Blaise Pascal was
nor Lorca
nor Kierkegaard
nor Gregory Corso
nor Amelia Earhart
nor Joni
nor Nico
nor Richie Havens
nor Levon Helm
but in the same pub
you told me so much
about yourself
my heart nearly burst

Belfast

on some plane tomorrow
with the whiskey
over Belfast

minature cars & farms
your lips are the clouds
cold longing in the sky

my eyes out the window
& the times we never touch
roaring with the engines

Errant

you're out beyond
the errant sky

far out
driving with Audrey
over the errant clouds

& you have a humbug
in your coat pocket
in case your mouth gets dry

& Audrey once shot through
the traffic lights at Larne
asking 'are there cars in Heaven?'

& if there weren't cars in Heaven
she didn't want to go there

but there are cars in Heaven
sure look at you both this Sunday morning
heading over the errant sky
for a big chicken dinner

The Other Place

everyday I speak to the dead
& sometimes they answer

I speak to the dead
about mundane things

like cupboards or spoons
& sometimes they answer

aye its a strange carry-on
me talking to the dead so much

the dead are at my table
they have full glasses

blue full glasses
the dead drink out of

are all over my kitchen
as the dead drink at my table

sure look there's Norbert!
but with no saxophone

there's Brian looking happier!
& perhaps there will be singing

singing & cajoling & toasting
when the dead sit at my table

myself & the dead
walk in the park

a silent procession
kicking the leaves

then they say it so urgently
'please don't stray

don't leave us alone'
& I look for sunken faces

the sunken faces of the dead
but there are none in the park

as they roll about in the leaves
the dead just feeling like a party

on a train to Durham with the dead
on a ship to Norway too

up this alleyway they follow
every underpass & junction

they wave their crazy flags
they make their animal noises

my constant companions
how I've grown to love each one

their invisible cloaks & bluster
how I've grown to love the dead

love lasts forever & let nobody persuade you otherwise

I'm a strong man
& love the damaged
I'm a saint

I repair & I cry
often in public
& I'm not ashamed

because it's worth it
in this menagerie
with its wars & money

& blood & flesh
its cankered apple
its cruel venom

its uncontrollable rain
its fantastic journeys
its flickering of lids

its dangerous games
its towerblocks
& rich girls who fly

& I think loving works
looking out for each other
mending stitches

stroking her cheek
or the note after twenty years
left in the coffee jar

'I love you' inside
cos I'm a survivor
of the scrapyard

of the hunger strikes
of the filthy war
of the bulldozers

& survivors have to breathe
& talk to the trees
& snap off the branch

& they have to know
Love lasts forever
& it's more real than milk

& somebody has to
stand up & say this
so I guess it's me

BIOGRAPHICAL NOTE

Brendan Cleary is originally from County Antrim, Ireland. He grew up at the height of the so-called "Troubles." His collection, *The Irish Card* (Bloodaxe Books, 1993), explores his sense of being an "inner émigré" following his move to England in the late seventies. He was the founder-editor of *The Echo Room* magazine and press and has been an abiding presence in the UK poetry scene for over thirty-five years. He has published many full-length collections and chapbooks and performed his poems extensively throughout Great Britain. Tall Lighthouse Press has just reissued *Goin' Down Slow: Selected Poems 1985–2010*. His last collection, *Face* from Pighog Press, was critically acclaimed. He has also published collections from Bloodaxe and Wrecking Ball Press. He lives and writes in Brighton where, until recently, he worked as a poetry tutor and Blues/Soul/Country DJ.